CONFERENCE PROCEEDINGS

T0302801

Perspectives of Chief Ethics and Compliance Officers on the Detection and Prevention of Corporate Misdeeds

What the Policy Community Should Know

Michael D. Greenberg

RAND Center for Corporate Ethics and Governance

A RAND INSTITUTE FOR CIVIL JUSTICE CENTER

This report results from the RAND Corporation's continuing program of self-initiated research. Support for such research is provided, in part, by the generosity of RAND's donors and by the fees earned on client-funded research. This research was conducted within the RAND Center for Corporate Ethics and Governance, which is part of the RAND Institute for Civil Justice, a unit of the RAND Corporation.

Library of Congress Cataloging-in-Publication Data is available for this publication.
ISBN 978-0-8330-4726-7

The RAND Corporation is a nonprofit research organization providing objective analysis and effective solutions that address the challenges facing the public and private sectors around the world. RAND's publications do not necessarily reflect the opinions of its research clients and sponsors.

RAND® is a registered trademark.

Cover photo courtesy of Noel Hendrickson/Lifesize Collection/Getty Images

Published 2009 by the RAND Corporation
1776 Main Street, P.O. Box 2138, Santa Monica, CA 90407-2138
1200 South Hayes Street, Arlington, VA 22202-5050
4570 Fifth Avenue, Suite 600, Pittsburgh, PA 15213-2665
RAND URL: http://www.rand.org/
To order RAND documents or to obtain additional information, contact
Distribution Services: Telephone: (310) 451-7002;
Fax: (310) 451-6915; Email: order@rand.org

PREFACE

On March 5, 2009, RAND convened a conference in Washington, D.C., on the role and perspective of corporate chief ethics and compliance officers (CECOs), in supporting organizations in the detection and prevention of corporate misdeeds. The conference brought together thought leaders from among ethics and compliance officers in the corporate community, as well as stakeholders from the nonprofit sector, academia, and government. Discussions focused on the challenges facing corporate ethics and compliance programs as a first line of defense against malfeasance and misbehavior; on the role of chief ethics and compliance officers as champions for implementation within their companies; and on potential steps that might be taken by government to empower chief ethics and compliance officers, and by extension, the corporate ethics and compliance programs that they oversee.

Improvements in corporate compliance, ethics, and oversight have been a significant policy goal for the U.S. government at least since the enactment of the U.S. Federal Sentencing Guidelines in 1991 and of the Sarbanes-Oxley Act in 2002. Notwithstanding these earlier legislative and regulatory initiatives, the collapse of financial markets in late 2008 has invited renewed questions about the governance, compliance, and ethics practices of firms throughout the U.S. economy. The purpose of the March 2009 RAND conference was to stimulate a broad discussion about companies' corporate ethics and compliance programs, drawing on the expertise of persons directly involved in marshaling and leading those programs. The discussion offers an important perspective and set of insights for government policymakers as they reflect on how best to respond to the economic crisis with new regulatory initiatives, and on how the institutional lever offered by CECOs can be employed to drive positive change within private-sector organizations.

These RAND conference proceedings summarize key issues and topics from the discussion sessions held on March 5. The document is not intended to be a transcript, and instead organizes the major themes of discussion by topic — in particular, pointing out areas of agreement as well as disagreement. With the exception of three invited papers that were written in advance, presented by conference participants, and are included without edit in an appendix to this document, we do not attribute any specific remarks to specific persons who participated in the conference.

These proceedings should be of interest to stakeholders with any connection to corporate ethics, compliance, and governance practices in the United States, and particularly to those responsible for crafting U.S. regulatory policy connected with these issues.

THE RAND CENTER FOR CORPORATE ETHICS AND GOVERNANCE

The Center for Corporate Ethics and Governance is committed to improving public understanding of corporate ethics, law and governance, and to identifying specific ways that businesses can operate ethically, legally, and profitably at the same time. The Center's work is supported by voluntary contributions from private-sector organizations and individuals with interests in research on these topics.

The Center is part of the RAND Institute for Civil Justice (ICJ), which is dedicated to improving decision-making on civil legal issues by supplying policymakers with the results of objective, empirically based, analytic research. The ICJ facilitates change in the civil justice system by analyzing trends and outcomes, identifying and evaluating policy options, and bringing together representatives of different interests to debate alternative solutions to policy problems. ICJ builds on a long tradition of RAND research characterized by an interdisciplinary, empirical approach to public policy issues and rigorous standards of quality, objectivity, and independence.

ICJ research is supported by pooled grants from corporations, trade and professional associations, and individuals; by government grants and contracts; and by private foundations. ICJ disseminates its work widely to the legal, business, and research communities and to the general public. In accordance with RAND policy, all ICJ research products are subject to peer review before publication. ICJ publications do not necessarily reflect the opinions or policies of the research sponsors or of the ICJ Board of Overseers.

James Dertouzos, Acting Director
RAND Institute for Civil Justice
1776 Main Street
P.O. Box 2138
Santa Monica, CA 90407–2138
310-393–0411 x7476
Fax: 310-451-6979
Jim_Dertouzos@rand.org

Michael Greenberg, Research Director
Center for Corporate Ethics and Governance
4570 Fifth Avenue, Suite 600
Pittsburgh, PA 15213-2665
(412) 682-2300 x4648
FAX: (412) 682-2800
Michael_Greenberg@rand.org

CONTENTS

SUMMARY

The worldwide economic collapse of 2008 has aroused the interest of U.S. policymakers in the mechanisms of corporate governance, compliance, and ethics, and their collective role in preventing and mitigating excesses and scandals in the corporate sector. Earlier rounds of corporate scandal gave rise to the Sarbanes-Oxley Act of 2002 (SOX) and to the Federal Sentencing Guidelines for Organizations in 1991, which reflected attempts to drive better corporate oversight and compliance through a combination of government mandates, incentives, and standard-setting. It remains to be seen whether the current financial meltdown in the U.S. mortgage and banking sectors will ultimately be attributable, in significant part, to failures in governance, compliance, and ethics. But regardless, 2009 is a year in which legislators and regulators are closely scrutinizing existing policy in these areas, with an eye toward addressing any lapses, loopholes, or inadequacies in the regulatory framework.

It is in this context that RAND convened a March 5, 2009, conference entitled "Perspectives of Chief Ethics and Compliance Officers on the Detection and Prevention of Corporate Misdeeds: What the Policy Community Should Know." The purpose of the conference was to draw on the perspectives and insights of chief ethics and compliance officers (CECOs) — senior corporate officials charged with responsibility for running compliance and ethics programs, and persons with a unique "insider" perspective on the challenges and opportunities involved in implementing them. The conference also included stakeholders with other, complementary viewpoints, including current and former legislative and executive branch officials, academics, and leaders from several nonprofit compliance and ethics associations. In convening this group for discussions about corporate ethics and compliance, the aim was to provide expert input to the policy community about the current state of ethics and compliance initiatives within corporations today — particularly as policymakers contemplate new avenues for regulatory oversight of corporations in the future.

Several major ideas emerged from the conference discussions. First was the observation that chief ethics and compliance officers occupy a unique position in corporate management, and in principle, they can be at least as important to successful ethics and compliance performance as are any of a host of programmatic initiatives like compliance hotlines, ethical codes of conduct, or formal training. In practice, the effectiveness of a CECO is likely to depend on how his or her specific role is defined, whether he or she has direct access to the board and to C-suite decisionmakers, and whether he or she oversees an ethics and compliance function that is independent of other corporate groups, such as legal or human resources. A second general theme arising from the conference was the importance of organizational culture, as a vital part of what a CECO is supposed to oversee. *Culture* refers to an intangible set of shared understandings about how a corporation operates and what its chief values are. To the extent that trust, honesty, and fairness become embodied in a company's brand promise and in the shared understanding of its workers, then that in turn can be a powerful prophylactic in avoiding misconduct. A third theme discussed extensively during the conference was the importance of open communication, internal whistleblowers, and employee reporting as major defenses against fraud and misconduct. Creating a culture of open communication, together with appropriate safeguards to encourage workers to come forward and protect them against retaliation, are additional important responsibilities for a CECO.

INVITED REMARKS FROM THREE PANELISTS

The initial session of the conference was dedicated to invited remarks from three panelists, all of them current or former CECOs or practitioners. The first panelist discussed a series of reasons for why many corporate compliance programs are "set up to fail" — arguably because those programs represent check-the-box efforts to meet legal requirements, without effective and committed leadership in implementing and managing them on a day-to-day basis within companies. The second panelist focused on the role of boards in oversight for compliance and ethics. He described the common law and regulatory requirements that establish directors' responsibilities in this arena, and then reflected on how directors can best fulfill their duties. This panelist suggested that here, again, the CECO can play a key role, as a designated management proxy who can provide the board with the information and access it needs in order to meet its own responsibilities for oversight. The third panelist presented a lengthy list of measures that government might consider undertaking to promote better ethics and compliance performance in corporations. Some of those steps could serve to empower ethics and compliance officers to be more effective within their organizations, while others involve a range of collaborative activities, training efforts, and/or incentives to corporations to implement better ethics and compliance programs.

CORPORATE COMPLIANCE, GOVERNANCE AND REGULATION — THE CECO PERSPECTIVE AND ROLE

The second session of the conference involved a moderated discussion on a broad range of issues connected with corporate governance, compliance, and regulation. The session opened with some reflections on the regulation of corporate governance and compliance, on the impact of SOX, and on the tension between stronger regulatory controls for corporations and the performance pressures for management to adopt a short-sighted, "meet-the-numbers" operating posture. Some but not all of the discussions touched on the central role of CECOs as drivers of the corporate compliance function, and as potential agents for boards of directors in carrying out the governance responsibilities of the latter. The reality that many corporate compliance programs fall short in achieving their aims was a major theme of conversation, with a serial focus on several of the different reasons why this appears to be so. When asked for potential top priorities for government intervention to improve corporate compliance and ethics efforts, one participant suggested that government place greater emphasis on acknowledging and rewarding positive ethics and compliance performance, as a complement to its ongoing enforcement and prosecution efforts against offenders. As another initial step, the participant also suggested that the government designate specific agency officials as formal leads and points of contact for the private sector on corporate ethics and compliance issues.

Major points of agreement in this discussion session included the following:

- CECOs have a very different role and perspective in their companies from that of chief counsel.

- CECOs have the potential to play a pivotal role in companies, but their effectiveness depends on independence, seniority, "seat at the table," and empowerment.

- Directors have significant responsibility for compliance oversight, but many are relatively unprepared, inexperienced, and/or ineffective in that role.

- Legal requirements and regulatory mechanisms can be important elements in driving corporate governance and compliance efforts, but mandates can sometimes also have perverse effects.

- Ethical culture is a prime responsibility for CECOs and a major factor in achieving good organizational compliance and ethics, but it is difficult to establish by external mandate.

CORPORATE CULTURE AND ETHICS — CONSIDERATIONS FOR BOARDS AND POLICYMAKERS

The final discussion session of the conference focused more deeply on the topics of corporate culture and ethics, their relationship to formal ethics and compliance initiatives, and considerations for boards and policymakers in trying to promote a strong ethical culture within organizations. Much of the discussion during this session focused on whistleblowing and the importance of an "open-communication" culture that encourages employees to raise concerns and report instances of malfeasance or misconduct to management. Whistleblowing presents a challenging set of practical and cultural issues for corporations to manage. On the practical side, these issues include implementing controls and mechanisms to support and protect workers who come forward as whistleblowers, while on the cultural side, the issues extend to creating an environment of trust and non-retaliation in which people feel comfortable with coming forward to disclose, even when this involves reporting misconduct committed by peers or superiors. Complementing the conference discussion about whistleblowing, this session also touched on a range of other issues connected with organizational culture and ethics, such as the formal definition of *corporate culture*, the return-on-investment argument in support of ethics and compliance activity, and the challenges involved in pressing the corporate community to take ethics and compliance — and the development of ethical culture within organizations — more seriously.

Several of the major points of discussion and agreement during the session included the following:

- Whistleblowing and open employee communication are critical resources for detecting fraud within companies.

- Anti-retaliation mechanisms are focal to efforts to protect whistleblowers, and by extension, to encourage them to come forward.

- Anti-retaliation ties directly to organizational culture and to norms about trust, honesty, and open communication.

- "Corporate culture" corresponds to a series of intangibles, including expectations of and about workers, ways of doing business, internal and external reputation, and other factors not captured by written policy.

- A return-on-investment argument for compliance and ethics (and for ethical culture) has been challenging to make, with the result that compliance and ethics may often be viewed by management as a cost center, rather than a revenue center.

- CEO endorsement of ethics as an overriding priority in an organization (or an industry) can sometimes help to drive top-down changes in culture and values.

ACKNOWLEDGMENTS

I wish to thank the panelists, speakers, and all those who engaged in the conference discussions, without whom the exchange of ideas documented here would not have been possible. I would particularly like to thank the current and former CECOs who participated in the conference, including Donna Boehme, Keith Darcy, Pat Gnazzo, Joe Murphy, Harold Tinkler, and Alan Yuspeh, as well as J. Troy Beatty of the Securities and Exchange Commission and Stephen Kohn of the National Whistleblowers Center. In addition, I would also like to thank Amy Coombe, Michelle Horner, and Jamie Morikawa from RAND for their assistance in every aspect of putting the conference together, managing logistics, capturing the discussions on the day of the event, and generating this proceedings document. *Per aspera ad astra.*

ABBREVIATIONS

C&E	compliance and ethics
CECO	chief ethics and compliance officer
CEO	chief executive officer
CFO	chief financial officer
DII	Defense Industry Initiative
DOJ	U.S. Department of Justice
FSGO	Federal Sentencing Guidelines for Organizations
ICJ	RAND Institute for Civil Justice
ROI	return on investment
SOX	Sarbanes-Oxley Act of 2002

1. INTRODUCTION

Improvements in corporate ethics, compliance, and governance have been a significant policy priority for the U.S. government over the past 20 years. In 1991, the U.S. Sentencing Commission promulgated a set of Federal Sentencing Guidelines for Organizations (FSGO) to guide judges in imposing appropriate penalties on corporate organizations whose employees commit federal crimes.[1] Notably, the FSGO included recommendations to organizations for establishing effective compliance mechanisms, which, if followed, also offer grounds for more lenient criminal sentencing by judges. Subsequent prosecutorial guidance materials issued by the U.S. Department of Justice (DOJ) in 2003,[2] and revisions to the FSGO in 2004, elaborated on the elements to consider in prosecuting and sentencing organizations, and placed emphasis on mitigating factors such as corporate cooperation and effective compliance efforts, the distinction between real and "paper" compliance programs, and the importance of establishing an ethical organizational culture. Meanwhile and in a complementary vein, the Sarbanes-Oxley Act of 2002 (SOX) introduced a series of substantive legal requirements for corporate compliance and disclosure, as with regard to internal control structures and reporting processes (§404), financial statement accuracy (§401), officer certifications (§302), and whistleblower protections (§806). Collectively, these various federal policies were intended to address perceived lapses and shortcomings in corporate oversight, and to create incentives and requirements for more effective self-policing by organizations.

In the wake of the Enron and WorldCom scandals of the early 2000s, it was hoped that SOX in particular would help to limit the occurrence of future waves of corporate malfeasance and ethical misbehavior. Limited empirical evidence addressing this point, however, has not been encouraging. Although a 2003 national telephone survey of American workers on ethical practices and workplace misconduct showed improvements on several measures from findings in earlier years,[3] the most recent follow-on survey in 2007 suggested that observed misconduct has now returned to pre-ENRON levels, and furthermore that many American workers choose not to report misconduct by co-workers out of fear of reprisal.[4] These sorts of findings are unsurprising, in light of newer rounds of corporate misbehavior that have occurred in recent years, including the stock options back-dating scandals and the mutual fund market-timing scandals of the mid-2000s. Of course, the most recent set of corporate scandals has broadly swept across the mortgage and banking sectors, in a series of events that culminated in the worldwide financial collapse of late 2008. It remains for history to judge what role corporate

---

[1] For discussion and history of the FSGO, see U.S. Sentencing Commission (undated).

[2] See Thompson (2003).

[3] See Ethics Resource Center (2003).

[4] See Ethics Resource Center (2007).

compliance, governance, and ethics truly played in the lead-up to the collapse. But what does seem clear is that the collapse has heralded a renewed interest among policymakers in these issues, as they consider new regulatory frameworks for the financial sector and other parts of the economy.

It is in this context that RAND convened a March 5, 2009, conference entitled "Perspectives of Chief Ethics and Compliance Officers on the Detection and Prevention of Corporate Misdeeds: What the Policy Community Should Know." The aim of the conference was to draw on the perspectives and insights of chief ethics and compliance officers (CECOs) — senior corporate officials charged with broad responsibility for ensuring that companies and their employees meet high standards of ethical and lawful behavior. Conference participants included current and former CECOs and practitioners, nonprofit leaders in fields related to corporate ethics and compliance, academics, and current and former legislative and executive branch officials. Discussions at the conference focused on the challenges facing corporate compliance and ethics (C&E) programs as a first line of defense against malfeasance and misbehavior; on the role of CECOs as champions for implementing C&E programs within their companies; and on potential steps that could be taken by government to empower CECOs, and by extension, to strengthen the corporate C&E programs that they oversee. Participants in the conference are listed in Appendix A of this document, while the conference agenda is reproduced in Appendix B.

Prior to the conference, three of the invited CECOs and practitioners were asked to prepare remarks on challenges currently facing corporate ethics and compliance officers and programs, the role of boards of directors in providing related oversight, and ways in which government might act to empower more effective C&E programs, and CECOs, within companies. These remarks were then presented in the initial session of the conference. A short summary of their remarks is presented in the next chapter of this document, and the written papers on which these remarks were based are reproduced in their entirety in Appendix C of this document.

The second session of the conference involved a moderated discussion on the topic of "Corporate Governance, Compliance, and Regulation: The CECO Perspective and Role." Chapter Three of this document provides a summary of the major themes and topics of conversation in this session.

The final session of the conference involved a moderated discussion on the topic of "Corporate Ethics and Culture: Role of Boards and Policymakers." Chapter Four of this document provides a summary of major themes and ideas that were discussed in this session.

2. INVITED REMARKS FROM CONFERENCE PARTICIPANTS

OVERVIEW

The conference began with remarks from three of the current and former CECOs and practitioners in attendance. Their remarks were based on invited, short papers on the topics "Why Many Corporate Compliance and Ethics Programs Are Positioned for Failure," "Ethics and the Role of the Board as Governing Authority," and "What Government Can Do to Help Prevent Corporate Crime." Printed in this chapter are summaries for each of these sets of remarks, written by their original authors. The invited papers are reprinted in their entirety in Appendix C of this document.

Summary of Remarks: From Enron to Madoff — Why Many Corporate Compliance and Ethics Programs Are Positioned for Failure
Donna Boehme, Compliance Strategists, LLC

Where Was the Ethics Officer?

Despite significant activity by companies to develop compliance and ethics programs over the past few decades, several studies have indicated that little progress has been made, and recent events in the corporate world suggest that effective mechanisms to prevent corporate misconduct are lacking. It is time for companies to get serious about corporate compliance and ethics — and a key initial step in achieving this involves the creation of a C-level, empowered compliance and ethics officer.

The "Kumbaya" Approach to Ethics and Compliance

Many current compliance and ethics programs suffer from the "Kumbaya" approach: An optimistic but rather naive expectation that once a code is published, a hotline activated, a rousing speech and memorandum from the chief executive officer (CEO) delivered, and an "ethics officer" appointed, then all the employees and managers will join hands in a "Kumbaya" moment, and the program will somehow magically work as envisioned. This kind of program may look good at first, but without continuing, empowered leadership on compliance and ethics issues, together with tangible management commitment to making hard choices, such a program is unlikely to succeed in preventing, detecting, and addressing real world problems.

Leading Integrity: The Critical Role of the Chief Ethics and Compliance Officer

An effective approach to integrity and corporate ethics starts with a senior-level CECO who understands the compliance and ethics field, is empowered and experienced, and has the independence, clout, a "seat at the table" where key senior management decisions are made, and resources to lead and oversee a company's ethics and compliance program - even when that program appears at odds with other key business goals of the company.

Policymakers Need to Support Effective Programs

Congress and regulators can also do more to support effective CECOs and (by extension) effective corporate ethics and compliance programs. More is needed from government and policymakers to more plainly state the expectations for an effective CECO and a strong corporate ethics and compliance program: Ultimately, prerequisites for protecting the interests of the organization itself, and for maintaining accountability to other stakeholders and to the public interest.

How Can Companies Put Integrity Back in Business?

Beyond the establishment of a serious, empowered CECO role to lead and oversee the program, there are a number of features viewed as essential indicia of a serious compliance and ethics program (i.e., one with "teeth"), including executive and management compensation linked to compliance and ethics leadership; integration of clear, measurable compliance and ethics goals into the annual plan; and direct access and periodic unfiltered reporting by the CECO to a compliance-savvy board.

Conclusion and Way Forward

Unless we want to keep asking, "Where was the ethics officer?", it is time for companies — and policymakers — to reject a check-the-box approach to ethics and compliance programs, and to get much more serious about putting integrity back into the heart of business.

Summary of Remarks: Ethics and the Role of the Board as Governing Authority
Keith Darcy, Ethics and Compliance Officer Association

Introduction: Can the Board Truly Oversee Compliance and Ethics?

The current financial crises and fresh wave of corporate scandals have put the spotlight back on the role of boards of directors in overseeing the activities of management. Legal and regulatory developments such as Caremark, the FSGO, and SOX have greatly increased the expectations on boards to oversee the compliance and ethics and culture of the companies they serve. This paper poses the threshold question: Can corporate boards, given the breadth and depth of their responsibilities, truly oversee ethics and compliance in their companies?

Management Support for the Board in Addressing Ethics and Compliance

An essential supporter to the board is the CECO, who acts as an agent for the board in meeting its regulatory and extra-regulatory responsibilities. Board-backed independence for the CECO can ensure that he or she has the appropriate authority to carry out his or her critical mandate, and by extension, to support the board in fulfilling its responsibility for ethics and compliance oversight.

Considerations for the Board in Fulfilling its Fiduciary Role

A board that is effective in overseeing ethics and compliance within a firm is armed with two key weapons: First, knowledge, and second, an empowered CECO. There are a number of specific ways that directors should consider discharging their oversight responsibilities for compliance and ethics:

- Directors must make time on the board agenda for periodic progress reports from the CECO.

- Boards should receive briefings on the highest compliance and ethics risks for the company and what the company is doing to address these risks. Periodic, if not continuous, risk assessment is essential.

- Directors should tell management and the CECO the important matters they want to hear about, and management should be responsive to the request — without exceptions, excuses, or filtering.

- Board members should make sure that the CECO is independent, empowered, connected, and professional. They should insist that the CECO be a senior, empowered member of management, with a proven track record in compliance and ethics, and with direct, unfiltered access to the board.

<u>Conclusion</u>

The board of directors' primary supporter in overseeing compliance and ethics within the company is the CECO. In addition to the "tone from the top" set by management and the engagement of the business at all levels, the CECO requires the strong support and involvement of the board of directors to achieve this purpose. And in turn, the directors can significantly enhance the discharge of their legal responsibilities for corporate compliance and ethics with the support of an effective agent in the person of the CECO.

Summary of Remarks: What Government Can Do to Help Prevent Corporate Crime
Joe Murphy, Society of Corporate Compliance and Ethics

Introduction

     While the CECO serves as the internal linchpin for driving corporate ethics and compliance efforts, government also has a major role to play in contributing to those efforts from the outside. Just as government initiatives such as the FSGO have already driven companies to take the first steps toward effective ethics and compliance programs, so too can government help to drive additional changes within companies, in an effort to fully charge the power of these programs. This paper offers a series of ideas and suggestions for further steps that government could take along these lines.

What Policy Options Might Government Consider?

1. Issue enforcement policy statements that recognize the importance of empowered CECOs in corporate compliance efforts
2. Publicize the benefits of strong leadership in compliance and ethics programs.
3. Establish practical, flexible standards for the CECO role.
4. Incorporate reference to CECOs into requirements for government procurement.
5. Incorporate reference to CECOs in deferred prosecution agreements, corporate integrity agreements, and other settlements.
6. Revise the FSGO.
7. Other regulatory agencies could address the potential role of CECOs in addressing specific areas of risk and compliance.
8. Encourage stock exchanges to consider the role of the CECO.
9. Factor the role of CECOs in administering voluntary disclosure programs.
10. Consider reducing regulatory requirements for companies with strong compliance programs and empowered CECOs.
11. Consider establishing the relevance of CECOs in compliance programs as a defense to civil liability.
12. Consider the CECO role as a defense for directors' liability.
13. Encourage extension of the CECO role through the supply chain.
14. Offer tax credits.
15. Establish conditions for access to government bailout money.
16. Participate actively in compliance and ethics conferences.
17. Obtain training for government officials.
18. Promote corporate compliance initiatives as a focal aspect of government oversight efforts.
19. Avoid anti-compliance actions and rulings.
20. Establish legal protection for corporate compliance efforts.

21. Provide a role model of a robust compliance and ethics approach: government agency compliance programs.
22. Collaborate with international organizations.
23. Evaluate the drawbacks, as well as the advantages, of mandatory compliance programs.
24. Designate an official in charge.
25. Establish credible program assessment.

Conclusion

As the foregoing list makes clear, there is a great deal that the government potentially could do to promote more effective corporate ethics and compliance programs, and in particular to empower the CECO as an agent of change. We respectfully suggest that the empowerment of CECOs might be a particularly cost-effective method for government to intervene in this area, because it leverages the ability of companies to self-police. The compliance and ethics profession stands ready to assist in this mission.

3. CORPORATE GOVERNANCE, COMPLIANCE, AND THE IMPACT OF REGULATION — THE CECO PERSPECTIVE AND ROLE

OVERVIEW

Participants in this session discussed a broad range of issues connected with corporate governance, compliance, and regulation. The session opened with some reflections on the regulation of corporate governance and compliance, on the impact of SOX, and on the tension between stronger regulatory controls for corporations and the performance pressures for management to adopt a short-sighted, "meet-the-numbers" operating posture. Some but not all of the discussions touched on the central role of CECOs, as drivers of the corporate compliance function and as potential agents for boards of directors in carrying out the governance responsibilities of the latter. The reality that many corporate compliance programs fall short in achieving their aims was a major theme of conversation, with a serial focus on several of the different reasons why this appears to be so. Session participants generally agreed on several points:

- CECOs have a very different role and perspective in their companies from that of chief counsel.
- CECOs have the potential to play a pivotal role in companies, but their effectiveness depends on independence, seniority, "seat at the table," and empowerment.
- Directors have significant responsibility for compliance oversight, but many are relatively unprepared, inexperienced, and/or ineffective in that role.
- Legal requirements and regulatory mechanisms can be important elements in driving corporate governance and compliance efforts, but mandates can sometimes also have perverse effects.
- Ethical culture is a prime responsibility for CECOs and a major factor in achieving good organizational compliance and ethics, but it is difficult to establish by external mandate.

CECOS PLAY A DIFFERENT ROLE FROM THAT OF CHIEF COUNSEL

Although CECOs often come from legal backgrounds and have sometimes previously held the office of corporate legal counsel, discussion underlined the fact that the CECO role is very different from the internal counsel role within most companies. Broadly speaking, legal counsel within a company operates to identify and reduce liability risks, across a spectrum of corporate operations, support functions, regulatory areas, etc. Moreover, legal counsel tends to be oriented toward parsing and understanding the technical requirements of different areas of law, and ensuring that the company can respond in ways that are both operationally and legally sound.

While there are some similarities to the CECO role, there are also major differences. In particular, the CECO role was described as being managerial rather than legal, as embodying the corporate "conscience," and as being that of the executive who serves to challenge a narrowly technical perspective on whether senior management decisions are "legal." In overseeing reporting hotlines and whistleblower protection mechanisms, e.g., the CECO may sometimes wind up on the opposite side from the corporate counsel (or the human resources executive), in suggesting that internal grievances be aired, corrective actions taken, and procedures followed impartially, even where the result is painful for senior management or for the company in the short-run. In principle, the CECO is supposed to be the voice for doing the right thing because it is the right thing to do, and for engaging management in asking questions about what is "right" in different situations. The CECO also serves as the voice to articulate the pragmatic reasons for trying to do the "right" thing, as by raising the question, "How would a particular course of management action look if published on the front page of the *Wall Street Journal?*"

The discussion about the distinctive role of the CECO also touched on the difference between the *compliance* function (i.e., ensuring that employees and the firm comply with applicable laws) and the *ethics* function (i.e., doing right, beyond the formal dictates of law). There was some difference of opinion expressed about the relative importance of these functions, and whether there are particular circumstances or industries in which the compliance and ethics functions are best served by being divided under separate officials. While some at the table advocated for this kind of split, and particularly for the role of a very strong compliance officer who stands up as an enforcer against senior management, others (including several of the CECOs present) noted that the current practice of many companies in combining these functions helps to avoid some highly undesirable consequences, such as creating silos or weakening the individual functions. Several at the table observed that the ethics function is a natural complement to compliance, in that the former is fundamentally proactive and involves building organizational values to prevent misconduct, while the latter has a strong reactive element (in responding to misconduct after it occurs). At least two of the CECOs present suggested that an official who oversees ethics and not compliance runs the risk of being dismissed as a "theologian," while one who oversees compliance and not ethics may be undermined in building trust and an effective ethical culture within the firm.

CECO EFFECTIVENESS DEPENDS ON INDEPENDENCE AND VOICE

One of the resounding themes of the conference was that many of the concrete elements of corporate compliance and ethics programs, such as codes of conduct, hotlines, and formal training, are unlikely to be effective in preventing corporate misbehavior absent an internal, executive champion in the management hierarchy — the CECO. In turn, several of the conference participants noted that the CECO only becomes an effective champion when positioned correctly to carry out his or her job. For example, as more than one conference participant suggested, if the CECO is going to serve as the prime delegate of the board of directors in carrying out the directors' responsibilities for compliance and ethics oversight, then it follows that the CECO needs to have direct access to the board. If the CECO is supposed to offer a point of view different from that of the legal department or the human resources department, then likewise it follows that the CECO needs to be independent of, and not subordinate to, those aspects of corporate management. If the CECO is going to help the executive officers of the company by bringing ethics and compliance concerns into the highest level of strategic decisionmaking, then it follows that the CECO needs to be a member of the executive team. On a related note, one conference participant observed that high-profile instances of corporate fraud have often directly involved the chief counsel, chief financial officer (CFO), and/or CEO of an organization. If detecting and preventing fraud within the executive suite is supposed to be a part of the CECO role, then that represents another reason for ensuring that the CECO has independent access to the board, as well as a seat at the senior management table.

What emerged from the conference discussion on this point was the idea of the CECO as a lever — someone with both responsibility and power to drive an ethics and compliance agenda on multiple levels throughout an organization. There are several stakeholder groups that potentially stand to benefit from drawing on that lever to improve corporate oversight, including both government regulators and boards of directors. But as with any other lever, the usefulness of a CECO in creating movement depends on how the managerial role is shaped, and on where the CECO is placed within the organization.

DIRECTORS PLAY A KEY ROLE IN COMPLIANCE OVERSIGHT, BUT INEXPERIENCE AND LACK OF FOCUS HAMPERS THAT ROLE

Another theme that emerged in conversation was the role that boards of directors can and should play in overseeing corporate compliance and ethics initiatives. On the one hand, it was noted that directors (and particularly those serving on audit committees) do have some explicit responsibility for these functions under SOX and the FSGO. On the other hand, it was also noted that many directors (1) are only tangentially familiar with ethics and compliance as a management function; (2) possess only limited vision into the corporations they serve, thus reining in their capacity to perform such oversight effectively; and (3) may see corporate ethics and compliance oversight as ancillary to their main role of protecting shareholder interests.

It was suggested that some of these limiting factors on director performance may improve over time, e.g., as directors receive more opportunities for formal ethics training, as CECOs become more empowered, and as more frequent reporting contacts occur between directors and CECOs on ethics and compliance issues. It was also observed, however, that there may be a chicken-and-egg problem connected with the oversight role of directors. Ultimately, effective CECOs and C&E programs depend on board support and engagement. But the support and engagement of a board depends on the directors being sophisticated and knowledgeable about their own responsibilities for compliance and ethics — which, in turn, may be difficult to foster in the first place, absent a strong CECO and C&E program. The conference discussion did not resolve how to address this tangle, although one participant did note that naming former CECOs to serve as directors on corporate boards offers one incremental step toward untying the knot.

LAW AND REGULATION MAY HELP TO FACILITATE CECOS AND C&E, BUT MANDATES CAN SOMETIMES HAVE PERVERSE EFFECTS

Conference participants expressed conflicting views on how government can best facilitate more effective compliance and ethics programs within corporations. Several of the CECOs present offered a long list of potential steps that various government agencies might contemplate in the future to try to empower CECOs, incentivize corporations, and establish more effective relationships between government and the professional C&E community. While many of those present at the conference agreed that government should consider taking some of these sorts of steps, others also noted that strong government mandates for corporate compliance (like those embedded in SOX) have sometimes operated to create a check-the-box mentality within corporations, which in some sense may be a self-sabotaging result. In this vein, conflicting opinions were expressed about the degree to which SOX has truly been successful in improving ethics and compliance performance within companies. Although some participants at the conference viewed government mandates and a strong regulatory hand as potentially weakening internal ethics and compliance efforts, others noted that many of the best corporate performers in C&E are companies that previously got into serious trouble with government enforcers and subsequently undertook significant internal reform efforts as a result.

When asked what the top priorities ought to be for government action on C&E in the future, one conference participant suggested that a strong priority would simply be for each of several executive branch agencies (e.g., the Securities and Exchange Commission, the Environmental Protection Agency) to designate a specific official as the agency lead for dealing with corporate ethics and compliance issues, and as a point of contact for CECOs in the private sector to engage. It was argued that this step by itself could help establish better lines of communication between industry and government, as well greater sophistication within the executive branch about C&E issues. Another suggested priority was for government to undertake more formal efforts to highlight and publicize strong performers in C&E as model corporate citizens. One conference participant suggested that this kind of positive recognition would offer an important "carrot" to complement the government's "sticks" in driving compliance and ethics activities. Finally and in a much narrower vein, it was also suggested that the FSGO (and by extension, DOJ) should specifically consider whether a CECO controls an independent budget for C&E activities, as an indicator for whether his or her underlying C&E program is truly independent and effective. Where the budget for C&E is folded into another aspect of corporate operations (e.g., human resources), it was argued that the result is likely to subordinate the ethics and compliance function to the agenda and concerns of other branches of management.

BUILDING A STRONG ETHICAL CULTURE IS A KEY ASPECT OF THE CECO ROLE

One of the recurring themes in the conference discussion was the importance of corporate ethical "culture" as a facet of a robust ethics and compliance program, and the role of the CECO as a guardian of that culture. Concretely, it was suggested that employee whistleblowing and anti-retaliation efforts are major aspects of corporate culture that fall within the domain of the CECO to oversee. Where workers are encouraged to come forward with reports of malfeasance, and anti-retaliation is pursued seriously and recognized as a priority within the firm, that in turn contributes to a shared set of organizational values about disclosure, honesty, and trust. More generally, it was observed that a well-positioned CECO has a unique lens for influencing and tracking the culture of the firm, with regard to compliance and ethics practice at all levels. Beyond the relationships with senior management and the board, the CECO also oversees ethics and compliance training, related reporting mechanisms, and investigation of incidents of misconduct and abuse. These various CECO functions offer a range of avenues for establishing tone and values within an organization, and for communicating to workers how ethics and compliance fit into the organizational mission and daily practice. On a complementary note, it was also pointed out that the CECO has responsibility to try to measure the tenor of ethical culture within the organization, through a variety of objective and qualitative methods (e.g., tracking complaints, violations, retaliation rates, plus employee surveys and interviews on values, beliefs, and assumptions concerning organizational ethics and compliance).

One of the subtle themes that emerged from the conference discussion was the tension between government's interest in promoting ethical corporate culture and the limits of government's ability to do so directly. Several conference participants observed that culture, like quality, is intangible — something that cannot be fully and directly captured through more concrete C&E steps like codes of conduct, reporting hotlines, or formal training programs. Rather, ethical corporate culture is built on the backbone of these sorts of concrete steps, together with effective implementation, and most importantly, committed leadership in the organization that promotes and models the ethics and compliance agenda on a day-to-day basis. To the extent that ethical corporate culture ultimately involves a set of assimilated values, it is in that sense the opposite of a check-the-box approach to meeting narrowly legalistic requirements for controls and governance, imposed from the outside. Again, some conference participants cautioned that strong government mandates concerning compliance and controls have the potential to encourage a check-the-box mentality, implicitly at the expense of ethical culture. On the other hand, it was suggested that empowered CECOs, at least in principle, can help to protect ethical culture and move companies in the opposite direction.

4. CORPORATE CULTURE AND ETHICS — CONSIDERATIONS FOR BOARDS AND POLICYMAKERS

OVERVIEW

Participants in the final session of the conference focused more deeply on the topics of corporate culture and ethics, their relationship to formal C&E initiatives, and considerations for boards and policymakers in trying to promote strong ethical culture within organizations. Much of the discussion during this session focused on whistleblowing, and on the importance of an "open-communication" culture that encourages employees to raise concerns, and report instances of malfeasance or misconduct to management. Whistleblowing presents a challenging set of practical and cultural issues for corporations to manage. On the practical side, these issues include implementing controls and mechanisms to support and protect workers who come forward as whistleblowers, while on the cultural side, the issues extend to creating an environment of trust and non-retaliation in which people feel comfortable with coming forward to disclose, even when this involves reporting misconduct committed by peers or superiors. Complementing the conference discussion about whistleblowing, this session also touched on a range of other issues connected with organizational culture and ethics, such as the formal definition of *corporate culture*, the return-on-investment (ROI) argument in support of C&E activity, and the challenges involved in pressing the corporate community to take both C&E, and the development of ethical culture within organizations, more seriously.

Several of the major points of discussion and agreement during the session included the following:

- Whistleblowing and open employee communication are critical resources for detecting fraud within companies.
- Anti-retaliation mechanisms are focal to efforts to protect whistleblowers within companies, and by extension, to encourage them to come forward.
- Anti-retaliation ties directly to organizational culture, and to norms about trust, honesty, and open communication.
- "Corporate culture" corresponds to a series of intangibles, including expectations for workers, ways of doing business, internal and external reputation, and other factors *not* captured by written policy.
- An ROI argument for C&E (and for ethical culture) is challenging to make, with the result that C&E may more often be viewed by management as a cost center, rather than a revenue center.
- CEO endorsement of ethics as an overriding priority in an organization (or an industry) may sometimes help to drive top-down changes in culture and values.

WHISTLEBLOWING AND OPEN COMMUNICATION ARE KEY RESOURCES FOR DETECTING CORPORATE FRAUD

Many of the conference participants agreed that a major trip-line for detecting misconduct or fraud within a corporation involves the corporate employees themselves. One conference participant discussed results from recent studies undertaken by PricewaterhouseCoopers (2007) and by the Association of Certified Fraud Examiners (2008), both of which suggested that employees may be the single most important internal corporate resource for identifying the occurrence of fraud. At the same time, another conference participant observed that management attitudes toward whistleblowing are often ambivalent at best, and that the "whistleblower" label frequently has very negative connotations attached to it. Several participants observed that corporate insiders who come forward to management to report misbehavior or wrongdoing often place themselves at risk by doing so. Another conference participant suggested that it was unsurprising, in this light, that recent national surveys have suggested that many employees who observe misconduct in the workplace may be unwilling to report it to management through formal channels.[5]

A number of related thoughts were offered by conference participants. One person suggested that internal C&E hotlines for employee reporting tend to be dominated by calls that do not involve actual whistleblowing, but instead human resources problems. In consequence, it was suggested that appropriate monitoring and channeling of calls is likely to be very important in running an effective hotline. Another participant pointed out that, according to a recent Ethics Resource Center survey, the majority of employees who actually do report on corporate misconduct choose to do so through their own supervisors or through higher management. This is a result that underlines the importance of establishing an organizational culture of "open communication" that goes beyond hotline reporting, and it also suggests that CECOs may be limited in their ability to detect and track whistleblowing activity purely through C&E hotlines. Finally, it was observed that people's willingness to come forward and report misconduct is probably affected by the incentives and disincentives associated with their doing so. To the extent that companies (and government) want to encourage workers to report problems, creating positive institutional incentives and recognition for reporting is likely to be important to that end.

ANTI-RETALIATION MECHANISMS ARE FOCAL TO ENCOURAGING WORKERS TO COME FORWARD

Building on the discussion of whistleblowing, conference participants generally agreed that protecting workers from retaliation is one of the most important functions that CECOs and C&E programs can perform. In particular, one conference participant asserted that once

---

[5] See Ethics Resource Center (2007).

retaliation has occurred within a company in a particular area of the business, compliance activity is effectively dead in that area. Another participant observed that it is rare to witness companies that have punished their own managers or officers for retaliatory acts. Still another participant noted that anti-retaliation efforts within companies, and the protection of whistleblowers, are intimately linked to many of the other functions that C&E programs and CECOs are supposed to carry out. Finally, several others suggested that it is easy to give lip service to anti-retaliation as a corporate priority, but much harder to set up effective institutional mechanisms to implement it. Here again, the theme of the empowered CECO was raised: It was suggested that only a CECO with an open line of communication to the board, independence from other management groups, and a seat at the executive table is likely to be able to drive a really effective anti-retaliation effort, and particularly so in instances where alleged misconduct affects senior managers within the firm. It was also suggested that getting a company to recognize the need for robust anti-retaliation efforts, particularly in the context of other allegations of corporate misbehavior, may sometimes demand external compulsion to achieve (as through a deferred prosecution agreement).

ANTI-RETALIATION AND WHISTLEBLOWER PROTECTION TIE DIRECTLY TO CORPORATE CULTURE, AND TO NORMS ABOUT HONESTY, TRUST, AND OPEN COMMUNICATION

In some basic respects, it was observed that an organization's commitment to anti-retaliation, and the specific steps taken by the CECO and management to make anti-retaliation real and effective, tie directly into building an ethical culture within the organization. Employees' willingness to come forward depends partly on perceptions about how the organization responds to people who report problems, whether there is the appearance of genuine respect among management for people who do so, and whether there are fair organizational procedures to investigate reports and safeguard the reporters. Where these things do exist, they contribute to an environment in which it is comparatively safe to be honest, and in which institutional expectations about reporting misconduct are clear and explicit. In turn, this also has the potential over time to contribute to a shared set of values for those who work within the organization — an understanding that honesty and open communication are prized and expected, that the organization takes internal misconduct seriously, and that it stands behind its own people when they police themselves and expose evidence of malfeasance. One participant at the conference observed that the best examples of firms with strong ethical culture incorporate a commitment to honesty in their "brand promise," both in how the firm does business with the outside world and in how the employees of the firm deal with each other. It was suggested that a serious commitment to anti-retaliation is one of the initial, fundamental building blocks for establishing that kind of organizational culture and brand promise.

ORGANIZATIONAL CULTURE IS A SERIES OF INTANGIBLES NOT CAPTURED BY FORMAL WRITTEN POLICY

One basic question that was posed in this session of the conference was "What is organizational culture?" Respondents agreed that culture within a firm corresponds to "the way things actually get done, regardless of what the written policy says," and more generally, the expectations of the firm with regard to its business, its people, and its reputation and brand promise. The idea of organizational culture as an "intangible" was reiterated, although several conference participants also suggested that culture is capable of being measured, at least indirectly, in several ways, and particularly through employee interviews and "the stories about the company that workers tell around the water-cooler." Building on the discussion from the first session of the conference, ethical culture was described as something that may emerge from concrete efforts to build strong C&E mechanisms (like formal training initiatives and codes of conduct), but that is not at all the same as those formal mechanisms. Ethical culture was also described as the end stage of what CECOs and C&E programs should be striving to monitor and achieve — not just implementing processes to obtain compliance, but cultivating an environment where workers and management internalize standards and values, in a way that ultimately helps to prevent the occurrence of misconduct in the first place.

Discussion touched again on the challenges for government in trying to promote this end, since external mandates can sometimes result in the opposite kind of organizational culture: a check-the-box orientation to satisfying the narrow dictates of the law. Here again, the conclusion of the group seemed to be that (1) incremental steps to empower CECOs may be the best way to move toward stronger ethical culture in organizations, and (2) focusing board and management attention on culture is one of the major roles that CECOs are in a unique position to perform.

ROI ARGUMENT FOR C&E, AND ETHICAL CULTURE, HAS BEEN DIFFICULT TO MAKE

Another topic that was raised in this session involved the challenge of making a strong, bottom-line argument for the value of C&E, and of ethical culture, to senior executives within a corporation. Several participants at the conference agreed that there is very limited empirical evidence currently available to demonstrate ROI as a function of particular C&E mechanisms or initiatives. Consequently, it was suggested that C&E may sometimes be regarded by senior executives as a cost center with few returns, for lack of ability to recognize or quantify the impact of C&E on brand and reputation, retention, deterrence of internal theft, avoidance of illegality and fines, etc. One implication discussed at the conference was the importance of constructing a salient and convincing business case for senior executives regarding the value of C&E, not purely in terms of the direct monetary return (which may be difficult to demonstrate), but more generally in terms of the amounts of money lost to fraud, impact on recruiting and retaining talent, and reputational effects. By implication, generating new empirical evidence to establish more directly the ROI of compliance and ethics activity could be of significant assistance to the business community, and it could make a compelling case for value to corporate officers and boards.

Conference participants were somewhat divided with regard to the perspectives that CEOs currently tend to bring to compliance and ethics initiatives. One participant suggested that CEOs need to look beyond the bottom line in recognizing the value of strong ethics and compliance programs. Otherwise, it was said, there is an inherent risk that compliance will be set aside whenever short-term returns can by improved by doing so. By contrast, another participant said that few CEOs need to be convinced that their companies need strong compliance programs to succeed, but that CEOs are often uncertain of what is required actually to achieve this, and that the value of pursuing ethics in addition to compliance is often far less clear to them.

TOP LEADERSHIP COMMITMENT CAN SOMETIMES DRIVE MAJOR CULTURAL SHIFTS IN FIRMS, AND EVEN ACROSS INDUSTRIES

One of the final questions raised in the discussion involved how CECOs can help move the corporate community at large toward a stronger commitment to ethics and compliance: In general, what is needed in order to get companies to take C&E more seriously? Beyond the ROI and business case arguments referred to earlier, one observation offered was that charismatic leadership can sometimes drive very significant cultural changes in organizations. One example given was that of Paul O'Neill (the former CEO of Alcoa) and his decision to pursue a zero-tolerance policy toward workplace accidents and serious injuries within his firm. It was suggested that over time, O'Neill's unequivocal commitment to this aim drove a basic cultural shift at Alcoa, as well as very substantial improvements in workplace safety there. In a similar vein, another participant observed that the Defense Industry Initiative (DII) provided an example where top leaders at several defense contractors came together, and because of their reputational concerns about perceived dishonesty, decided to drive a top-down commitment within their companies to pursue better ethics and compliance practices. Conference discussion suggested that the DII effort was successful in significant measure, and driven primarily not by legal concerns, but rather by customer management concerns and by the commitment of the chief executives to achieve better practice.

Another participant in the conference observed that at most companies, there is no analogous champion for corporate ethics and compliance at the very top level of management. It was suggested that this kind of leadership can indeed be an important driver of organizational change, but that it is not the kind of thing that external regulators can contribute to directly. Here again, the implication was that, as with empowering CECOs, building commitment of chief executives (and of boards of directors) to ethics and compliance is an important lever for changing the way that companies operate. There was no consensus on how to drive this kind of top-level commitment more broadly, although one person did note that CECO empowerment reflects an initial step in this direction, while another pointed out that corporations that have gotten into trouble under the FSGO (for example) have sometimes become leaders in executive commitment to C&E in the aftermath.

APPENDIX A: CONFERENCE PARTICIPANTS

Name	Affiliation
Moderator	
Michael D. Greenberg	Research Director, RAND Center for Corporate Ethics and Governance
Participants	
J. Troy Beatty	Senior Counsel, U.S. Securities and Exchange Commission
Donna Boehme	Principal, Compliance Strategists, LLC; Advisory Board Member, RAND Center for Corporate Ethics and Governance
Keith Darcy	Executive Director, Ethics and Compliance Officer Association
Paula J. Desio	Chair for Ethics Policy, Ethics Resource Center
Kathleen Getz	Senior Associate Dean for Academic Affairs, Kogod School of Business, American University
Pat Gnazzo	Senior VP and General Manager, U.S. Public Sector, CA, Inc.
Patricia Harned	President, Ethics Resource Center
Eric Helland	Senior Economist, RAND ICJ
Fred Kipperman	Associate Director, RAND ICJ
Stephen Kohn	President, National Whistleblowers Center
Gerald S. Martin	Visiting Assistant Professor, Kogod School of Business, American University
Joe Murphy	Public Policy Chair, Society of Corporate Compliance and Ethics
Edward Soule	Associate Professor, McDonough School of Business, Georgetown University
Harold Tinkler	Chief Ethics and Compliance Officer, Deloitte LLP
Alan Yuspeh	Senior VP, Chief Ethics and Compliance Officer, HCA, Inc.
Dean A. Zerbe	National Managing Director, alliantgroup

APPENDIX B: CONFERENCE AGENDA

12:50 pm Arrival and Registration

1:00 pm Welcome and Introductory Remarks
        Lynn Davis, Senior Fellow and Director, RAND Washington Office
        Michael Greenberg, RAND Corporation

1:10 pm Invited Remarks from Three Panelists

- From Enron to Madoff: Why Many Corporate Compliance Programs are Positioned for Failure
  Donna Boehme, Compliance Strategists, LLC

- Ethics and the Role of the Board as Governing Authority
  Keith Darcy, Ethics & Compliance Officer Association

- What Government Can Do to Help Prevent Corporate Crime
  Joe Murphy, Society of Corporate Compliance and Ethics

2:00 pm Discussion Session #1: Corporate Governance, Compliance, and the Impact of Regulation — The CECO Perspective and Role

- Introductory Remarks: J. Troy Beatty, U.S. Securities and Exchange Commission

---

3:15 pm Break

3:25 pm Discussion Session #2: Corporate Ethics and Culture — Role of Boards and Policymakers

- Introductory Remarks: Stephen Kohn, National Whistleblowers Center

---

4:40 pm Closing Remarks
        Michael Greenberg, RAND Corporation

APPENDIX C: INVITED PAPERS FROM PANEL PARTICIPANTS

From Enron to Madoff: Why Many Corporate Compliance and Ethics Programs Are Positioned for Failure
Donna Boehme, Compliance Strategists, LLC
Remarks presented on March 5, 2009

Introduction: "Where Was the Ethics Officer"?[1]

With the wreckage of the first generation of Enron-type corporate scandals in the rear view mirror, and the chaos of Madoff and the subprime meltdown now all around us, commentators are asking "Where were the ethics officers?" and "Are corporate compliance and ethics programs just window dressing?" These are fair questions, given that in the 18 years since the 1991 promulgation of the U.S. Organizational Sentencing Guidelines (which set out the roadmap for companies to detect and prevent wrongdoing),[2] several studies have indicated that little progress has been made,[3] and recent events in the corporate world suggest that effective mechanisms to prevent corporate misconduct are lacking. This paper sets out a response to these two questions from some leading practitioners in the field of corporate compliance and ethics. This paper also suggests a path forward, moving beyond the sometimes unrealistic assumption of policymakers, boards and management that integrity and compliance can be achieved simply by establishing basic elements such as a formal code of conduct, an "ethics officer," a training program, monitoring, and/or an employee helpline, and then expecting that good results will necessarily follow. In short, we believe that it is time for companies to get serious about corporate culture, accountability, compliance and ethics, and that the key initial step in achieving this involves the creation of a C-level, empowered compliance and ethics officer: someone with the experience, positioning, mandate and clout to actually make things happen in the organization.

---

[1] For convenience, the term "ethics officer" is intended to encompass the role of the chief compliance and ethics officer, in its many variations.

[2] The guidelines, including the 2004 amendment, are available at http://www.ussc.gov/guidelin.htm. The amendment became effective on November 1, 2004.

[3] The Ethics Resource Center's 2007 National Business Ethics Survey, based upon interviews with 2,000 employees at a broad range of public and private U.S. companies, found "little if any meaningful reduction in the enterprise-wide risk of unethical behavior at U.S. companies." ERC Press Release, November 28, 2007, available at http://www.ethics.org/about-erc/press-releases.asp?aid=1146.

The "Kumbaya" Approach to Ethics and Compliance

On paper, many companies have established a wide range of compliance and ethics programs since 1991.[4] Moreover, companies were subsequently required to add to their compliance infrastructure by Sarbanes-Oxley in 2004, and by other government efforts to impose elements of compliance programs. Today, most major corporations have at least some compliance and ethics infrastructure, including formal codes of conduct and confidential employee hotlines, and the new management role of "chief ethics and compliance officer" (CECO) is rising in demand. Most companies in highly regulated industries, such as financial services, health care, and defense, also have developed detailed compliance procedures. But there is a critical distinction between compliance and ethics programs that have all the designated features on paper, and those that have real "teeth" and the potential for success. The former might be described as adopting a "Kumbaya"[5] approach — an optimistic but rather naive expectation that once a code is published, a hotline activated, a rousing speech and memorandum from the CEO is delivered, and an "ethics officer" appointed, then all the employees and managers will join hands in a "Kumbaya" moment, and the program will somehow magically work as envisioned. This kind of program may look good at first, but without continuing, empowered leadership on compliance and ethics issues, together with tangible management commitment to making hard choices, such a program is unlikely to succeed in preventing, detecting, and addressing real world problems. We would note that Enron had a 64-page code of ethics and an employee hotline in place prior to the exposure of the scandals that ultimately brought that company down. Similarly, today's newspaper headlines are full of allegations of corporate fraud and crime, at companies with relatively hollow, check-the-box compliance and ethics programs.

Leading Integrity: The Critical Role of the Chief Ethics and Compliance Officer

We believe an effective approach to integrity and corporate ethics starts with a senior-level chief ethics and compliance officer (CECO) who understands the compliance and ethics field, is empowered and experienced, and who has the independence, clout, a "seat at the table" where key senior management decisions are made, and resources to lead and oversee a company's ethics and compliance program — even when that program appears at odds with other key business goals of the company. A well-implemented compliance and ethics program doesn't spring from the void ex nihilo — it requires a strong leader to engage others in the

---

[4] The U.S. Sentencing Guidelines, requiring organizations to establish an "effective program" to prevent and detect violations of law, were initially promulgated in 1991 and further amended in 2004. See footnote 2.

[5] Kumbaya, a 1930s Southern spiritual that some trace to the former slaves living in the sea islands of South Carolina and Georgia, is sometimes used to describe a "naively optimistic view of the world and human nature" — see http://en.wikipedia.org/wiki/Kumbaya.

organization, including powerful senior managers, to surface and resolve issues and challenges, and to make a culture of transparency, accountability and responsibility a reality.

But accomplishing this is easier said than done. To a great extent, the evolving role of the CECO was initially viewed by companies as a lower-level management or even administrative role, often positioned within the legal department or another function such as finance, audit or even HR, and with little empowerment, mandate or independence to fulfill the important accountabilities of the role. When compliance programs have been mandated by government rules and regulations, programs have tended to devolve into hyper-technical efforts devoid of senior-level participation and commitment.

In a serious compliance and ethics role, the CECO is often required to challenge the established way of doing things, or to introduce new concepts such as stricter controls on senior managers, increased transparency, and consistent standards of discipline. Imagine a CECO being called into the office of a powerful Andy Fastow-type CFO and being ordered to drop a confidential investigation, change a report to the Board, or otherwise compromise the responsibilities of the role. This is corporate ethics' "dirty little secret": In many companies today, the CECO is still poorly positioned, and lacking in the empowerment and independence needed for successful discharge of the critical role he or she is expected to play.[6] It is important to note that the "expectations" of having an effective CECO and ethics and compliance program come, not only from the organization itself, but also from regulators, from policymakers and other stakeholders, and from the general public.

This view is expressly endorsed by a startlingly candid white paper published last year on the topic, entitled "Leading Corporate Integrity: Defining the Role of the Chief Ethics and Compliance Officer" — a collaboration of five leading nonprofit organizations supporting the profession.[7] Echoing the sentiment that "most CECOs do not believe they have been given sufficient authority and resources to achieve their mission," the white paper comments that "many executives and boards have not yet realized the potential of their CECOs" and that "a CECO that serves as window dressing likely does more harm than good, especially in times of difficulty." The CECO's line of reporting is the "single biggest influence on his or her credibility within the organization" and should be a direct reporting relationship to either the CEO or the board, with "direct, unfiltered access to the Board." The CECO must be "independent to raise matters of concern without fear of reprisal or a conflict of interest." Further, a reporting line to the general counsel, one of the most common structures in

---

[6] As reported by the *Financial Times* on June 29, 2007, "Siemens Anti-Graft Chief Quits," Daniel Noa, a former German prosecutor with "impeccable credentials" appointed to the post as part of Siemens' response to the corruption scandal in 2007, quit the role involuntarily after only six months on the job. The paper quoted one source: "He was alone and lacked support. He came up against a lot of people who didn't want him to succeed in his job." Media reports cite a changed reporting relationship that "undermined" Noa, "infighting" and "lack of support."

[7] See Ethics Resource Center (2007), *Leading Corporate Integrity: Defining the Role of the Chief Ethics and Compliance Officer (CECO)*. This report is available for download at http://www.ethics.org/CECO/.

companies today, is not viewed as effective positioning — since the aim of reducing external litigation risk is not always well-aligned with the aim of promoting ethics and compliance within the organization. Thus for companies serious about integrity, merely establishing a new ethics management position is not sufficient as a foundation for a strong compliance and ethics program. Rather, close attention must also be paid to empowerment, mandate, a seat at the table, independence, and reporting relationships of the CECO. Without proper positioning, a CECO (and ultimately, the compliance and ethics program that he or she administers) is likely to be ineffective and in serious danger of failure.

That brings us back to the two questions we posed in the introduction, with regard to the most recent wave of corporate scandals: Question: "Where was the ethics officer?" Answer: "Present, but most likely lacking empowerment, positioning and independence (and probably not even a true 'officer' of the corporation)." Question: "Are corporate compliance and ethics programs just window-dressing?" Answer: "In many companies, probably yes."

Policymakers Need to Support Effective Programs

Congress and regulators can also do more to support effective CECOs, and (by extension) effective corporate compliance and ethics programs. For instance, the New York Stock Exchange (NYSE) listing rules have been hailed for requiring all listed companies to have a code of ethical conduct. This is certainly an important starting point in establishing a good compliance and ethics program, but by itself, a formal code of conduct can become an empty gesture unless that code is implemented effectively. Similarly, the Sarbanes-Oxley reforms of 2002 responded to a stream of corporate accounting and fraud scandals by mandating new ethics hotlines, codes of conduct, and stronger internal controls and reporting efforts, but here again, these steps are only part of the overall compliance and ethics approach needed to support a culture of integrity at a corporation. Two key ideas have been missing from related government regulations. First, any single element of a corporate compliance and ethics program, taken in isolation, is unlikely to be effective by itself. Thus, formal codes of conduct, employee hotlines, and internal controls ideally should all be implemented as parts of an overall, holistic compliance and ethics program. Second, such programs should ideally be led and overseen by a senior-level, empowered chief compliance officer, with the clout and independence to make things happen in the organization. Without both of these elements, an NYSE-style paper requirement for a formal code of conduct (for example) is unlikely to succeed in achieving its aims. In sum, more is needed from government and policymakers to make more plainly stated the expectations for an effective CECO and a strong corporate compliance and ethics program — ultimately, prerequisites for protecting the interests of the organization itself, and for maintaining accountability to other stakeholders and to the public interest. In a companion paper in this document (titled "What Government Can Do to Prevent Corporate Crime"), our colleague provides some specific suggestions on how policymakers can help to support more effective ethics and compliance programs and stronger CECOs.

How Can Companies Put Integrity Back In Business?

Perhaps the underlying question here is, how do we move beyond corporate compliance and ethics programs that look good on paper, but that are ineffective at achieving real world results? More generally, CEOs of successful companies know that little is accomplished in business without first having a plan, resources, and an accountable, effective leader in place to implement the plan. A company's program for compliance and ethics is no different from any other aspect of business enterprise. Where the stated goal is to change the culture of an entire organization, to identify and address key compliance and ethics risks, and to encourage good business judgments among all managers and employees, a serious approach and commitment of resources is needed. We've already described the first step of creating an empowered, independent CECO position, filling it with someone who is knowledgeable about compliance and ethics, and giving that person a seat at the senior management table. The rest of the formula, which the CECO will drive, has to do with implementing and integrating a range of compliance and ethics initiatives, supported by management at all levels of the organization. Without diminishing the key role of formal codes of conduct and help lines, establishing those features is a relatively easy part of a company's compliance and ethics effort. The more difficult aspects of the effort involve incorporating the company's code of conduct and policies into the DNA of its business operations, and all of the resulting tough choices management needs to make along the way in doing so. This is where many compliance and ethics efforts fall short, whether by lack of management resolve, loss of focus, or lack of leadership by a strong CECO in driving the program on a daily basis. Here are some examples of features we view as essential indicia of a serious compliance and ethics program (i.e., one with "teeth"):

- Executive and management compensation linked to compliance and ethics leadership
- Consistent enforcement of the company's code of conduct and policies, especially at senior levels
- Confidential, professional management of the help line, including investigations
- Vigorous enforcement of non-retaliation policies
- Effective and ongoing compliance and ethics risk-assessment
- Integration of clear, measurable compliance and ethics goals into the annual plan
- Direct access and periodic unfiltered reporting by the CECO to a compliance-savvy board
- Strong compliance and ethics infrastructure throughout all parts of the business
- Real compliance audits designed to uncover lawbreaking
- Practical and powerful action (not merely words) by the CEO and management team to promote compliance and ethics
- Shared learning within the company based on actual disciplinary cases.

Conclusion and Way Forward

With committed management support, together with empowerment, independence, a seat at the table, resources and appropriate reporting structure for its CECO, a company can forge beyond window-dressing in its compliance and ethics effort. This is an essential first step toward establishing a corporate culture of transparency, openness and integrity, in which ethical and compliance problems are more likely to be detected earlier rather than later — so that the company can seek to prevent fires, rather than put them out after the fact. Unless we want to keep asking "Where was the ethics officer?", it's time for companies — and policymakers — to reject a check-the-box approach to compliance and ethics programs, and get much more serious about putting integrity back into the heart of business.

Ethics and the Role of the Board as Governing Authority
Keith Darcy, Ethics and Compliance Officer Association
Remarks presented on March 5, 2009

Introduction: Can the Board Truly Oversee Compliance and Ethics?

The role of corporate directors in overseeing the activities of management has changed dramatically over the past several years. The days of director complacency are long gone. Shareholder activism has fostered greater scrutiny on director oversight responsibilities, with more emphasis placed on fostering corporate ethics, compliance and culture. At the same time, legal and regulatory developments have greatly increased expectations of directors in their oversight role.

The shift toward greater legal burdens for directors arguably began with the Caremark decision[1] in 1996, which elaborated on directors' oversight responsibilities in connection with fiduciary duty, and opened directors to personal liability in the event that they fail in fulfilling those responsibilities. In 2002, the Sarbanes-Oxley Act (SOX)[2] was passed, following the headline-grabbing scandals at Enron, Tyco, Xerox, Rite-Aid, Adelphia, HealthSouth, Arthur Andersen, Hollinger and WorldCom. Among other things, SOX clarified the board's accountability to ensure that adequate internal controls are in place within their companies. More recently, the 2004 amendments to the Federal Sentencing Guidelines expressly contemplate a board's obligation not only to exercise "reasonable oversight" but to "be knowledgeable" about its company's compliance and ethics activities.

Notwithstanding these and other changes in law and regulation affecting corporate directors, in the years since SOX there has been a series of further scandals and settlements involving Wall Street analysts, mutual funds, as well as the insurance, healthcare and pharmaceutical industries. Beyond the scandals in these specific industries, many other corporate directors have been taken to task for their role in scores of options back-dating schemes. And in early 2009, the directors of many large financial institutions are being criticized and subjected to intense regulatory and shareholder scrutiny, in connection with alleged failures in corporate management that may have contributed to the economic collapse. For example, the newly appointed Chair of the Securities and Exchange Commission, Mary Schapiro, has announced she will examine the role of directors during the economic meltdown, including their backgrounds, skills and how they managed issues like financial risk and executive compensation.[3] The juxtaposition of increasing legal responsibility of boards, together with their colorful track record in scandals in recent years, leads us to a pose a

---

[1] In re Caremark International Inc. Derivative Litigation, 698 A.2d 959 (Del. Ch. 1996)
[2] Sarbanes-Oxley Act of 2002 (Pub.L. 107-204, 116 Stat. 745, enacted July 30, 2002)
[3] "SEC to Examine Boards' Role in Financial Crisis," *Washington Post*, February 20, 2009.

fundamental question: Can corporate boards, given the breadth and depth of their responsibilities, truly oversee ethics and compliance in the companies they serve?

We would suggest that the appropriate answer is "yes." Directors are essentially "guardians" of a firm, charged with overseeing management to ensure that the firm's business is conducted with sound strategy and prudence. More than just maximizing return on investment, good governance demands that directors do everything in their power to protect shareholders' assets. Increasingly, too, various external stakeholders outside the company are raising questions about how a company conducts its social responsibilities. Consonant with these varied perspectives and responsibilities, directors' attention to the ethics and compliance function within their companies is an integral aspect of carrying out their fiduciary duty. This paper highlights the critical role of the board in overseeing the management of ethics within the company, and suggests some ways in which directors can most effectively discharge this critical duty of care.

Management Support for the Board in Addressing Ethics and Compliance

As a starting point, it is well understood that a corporate board cannot oversee the affairs of its company in a vacuum. Certain key executives have basic responsibilities to inform and assist the board in the discharge of their oversight duties, including the CEO, CFO, director of human resources and internal auditor. In the critical area of compliance and ethics, an essential supporter to the board is the chief ethics and compliance officer (CECO), who acts as an agent for the board in meeting its regulatory and extra-regulatory responsibilities. The role of the CECO in supporting the board is implicitly recognized in the U.S. Organizational Sentencing Guidelines,[4] which set up the roadmap for effective corporate compliance and ethics programs, and include, among other requirements:

- That the "governing authority" of a company must be knowledgeable and reasonably oversee the company's ethics and compliance program;
- That there must be a "high-level" person charged with oversight for the ethics and compliance program;
- That this individual must have adequate resources and appropriate authority to execute his/her responsibilities; and
- That the firm must take reasonable steps to communicate appropriate behaviors, and conduct effective training in compliance and ethics: including training aimed at the "governing authority."

[4] The Organizational Sentencing Guidelines (OSG) were originally promulgated by the U.S. Sentencing Commission in 1991, and then substantially amended in 2004. For a short summary describing the history and impact of the OSG, see discussion at http://en.wikipedia.org/wiki/Compliance_and_ethics_program.

Beyond the responsibilities set out for directors under the OSG, SOX also introduced new standards of accountability for directors of U.S. public companies (and foreign companies listed on U.S. stock exchanges). For example, under Section 406 of SOX, public companies must either explain why they have no code of conduct or else institute a code of ethics for senior financial officers to promote "honest and ethical conduct, including the handling of actual or apparent conflicts-of-interest between personal and professional relationships...fair, accurate and timely disclosure...and compliance with laws and regulations." In addition, Section 806 of SOX provides whistleblower protection "prohibiting discrimination in the terms of employment by public corporations, or any officer, employee, contractor, sub-contractor or agent of such corporation..." against insiders who blow the whistle internally on certain types of corporate misconduct. Finally under SOX, internal controls are now the direct responsibility of directors, and the failure to establish adequate institutional safeguards against misconduct carries significant personal risks and liability to the directors.

Given the many internal and external issues potentially impacting a company's reputation, how does a director protect shareholders' assets? More to the point: How do directors minimize a company's ethical liabilities and maximize its ethical assets?

Again, the logical starting point is in the person of a company's chief ethics and compliance officer: The CECO acts as an agent of the board in meeting its fiduciary obligations for oversight of corporate ethics. As pointed out by colleagues in two companion papers included in this report, a CECO must be a "chief," an executive-level officer reporting to the board of directors and involved in the strategic and policy decisions of the firm. Events of the recent past indicate that top executives like the CEO, CFO, general counsel and other senior officers frequently show up in the reports of the Federal Fraud Task Force. It is unlikely that a lower-level employee would have the clout to intervene at that level of management, let alone be privy to decisions being made in the "C suite." The CECO must be part of the company's power structure to be effective as an agent of the directors.

Independence of the CECO is also critical to ensuring that the ethics and compliance function is carried out effectively. Direct line reporting by the CECO to the board is a basic step toward ensuring that independence. In at least some companies, the board has direct oversight in hiring, firing, determining benefits and compensation for, and the responsibilities of, the CECO. Independence can be further assured by providing the CECO an employment contract, ample severance, indemnification, and full D&O insurance coverage. Where the CECO does not have a direct report to the board, a senior empowered position, direct access and the ability to make periodic, unfiltered reports to the board are important indicia of independence. Board-backed independence can ensure the CECO has the appropriate authority to carry out her mandate, and by extension, to support the board in fulfilling its responsibility for ethics and compliance oversight.

Considerations for the Board in Fulfilling Its Fiduciary Role

A board that is effective in overseeing ethics and compliance within its firm is armed with two key weapons: first, knowledge, and second, an empowered CECO. Some related aspects of fiduciary duty that directors should consider include the following:

- Board members must understand the risks they undertake in their role as fiduciaries, and how these risks can be mitigated or resolved.

- They must know and perform diligently their fiduciary responsibilities to oversee and be knowledgeable about the company's compliance and ethics program.

- Directors must make time on the board agenda for periodic progress reports from the CECO.

- Boards should receive briefings on the highest compliance and ethics risks for the company, and what the company is doing to address these risks. Periodic, if not continuous, risk assessment is essential.

- Directors should tell management and the CECO the important matters they want to hear about, and management should be responsive to the request — without exceptions, excuses, or filtering.

- Board members should make sure that the CECO is independent, empowered, connected and professional. They should insist that the CECO be a senior, empowered member of management, with a proven track record in compliance and ethics, and with direct, unfiltered access to the board.

- Directors should ask the CECO during every closed executive session — or even over coffee or at lunch — "What are you personally worried about or think we should know?"

- Directors should require that any CECO termination be approved by the board before management does anything, and be available for an exit interview.

- Directors should ask the CEO and the rest of the senior management team to tell them in person what specific things they do to promote ethics and compliance and support the CECO — in other words, demonstrate "how they walk the walk."

- Board members should periodically require a benchmark assessment regarding how the company's ethics and compliance program compares with that of other leading peer companies — is the company the leader, middle of the pack, or lagging behind?

Conclusion

Clearly, one of the most lethal threats to any organization is misconduct within its own ranks or in how it engages with the public. Ideally, we need to embed a system of values, ethics and compliance into the cultures of our organizations. The absence of these foundational values, especially in these frightening times, can only contribute to anomie, cynicism, despair, and in the end, continuing corruption within capitalist institutions. The CEO and senior management have primary responsibility for setting the tone, values and standards of behavior for the company. But as our colleague in a companion paper in this document has pointed out ("From Enron to Madoff: Why Many Corporate Compliance and Ethics Programs Are Positioned for Failure"), a compliance and ethics program cannot implement itself. It is the CECO who serves as the pivotal figure and architect in leading a program that supports a culture of integrity throughout the organization. In addition to the "tone from the top" set by management and the engagement of the business at all levels, the CECO requires the strong support and involvement of the board of directors to achieve this purpose. And in turn, the directors can significantly enhance the discharge of their legal responsibilities for corporate compliance and ethics with the support of an effective agent in the person of the CECO.

What Government Can Do to Help Prevent Corporate Crime

Joe Murphy, Society of Corporate Compliance and Ethics

Remarks presented on March 5, 2009

The current financial crisis and fresh round of corporate scandals[1] have led many observers to question whether enough is being done within U.S. companies to prevent corporate crime. In 1991, the Organizational Sentencing Guidelines promised companies that effective compliance and ethics programs would be recognized, and that companies making a serious commitment to preventing misconduct would benefit from doing so. Now, 18 years later, although the majority of large organizations have codes of conduct and some ethics infrastructures in place, progress in achieving better corporate ethics and compliance outcomes has been slow. A 2007 survey indicated that "[s]ix years after high-profile corporate scandals rocked American business, there has been little if any meaningful reduction in the enterprise-wide risk of unethical behavior at U.S. companies."[2] The ongoing parade of corporate crimes and ethical lapses certainly suggests that not enough has been done to press for strong ethics and compliance programs within companies.

As discussed in a companion paper in this report, we believe that one of the keys for success is having a fully empowered champion for these programs in every company — the chief ethics and compliance officer (CECO). In too many companies today, the ethics and compliance effort has either been incomplete in its design, or ineffective in its implementation and resourcing. A strong CECO can help to provide the impetus and focus to push company programs to a level where they actually work.

While the CECO serves as the internal linchpin for driving corporate ethics and compliance efforts, government also has a major role to play in contributing to those efforts from the outside. The Federal Sentencing Guidelines demonstrate the role of government standards in helping to establish corporate ethics and compliance programs. We observe, however, that although the guidelines' formula for compliance and ethics programs has many strong points, it also has some shortcomings and ambiguities. In particular, the guidelines' formula does not do enough to ensure the authority, resources and effectiveness of CECOs. As a result, the guidelines may fall short in ensuring the ability of companies to actually succeed in detecting and preventing wrongdoing.

In sum, just as government initiatives such as the Sentencing Guidelines have already driven companies to take the first steps toward effective ethics and compliance programs, so too can government help to drive additional changes within companies, in an effort to fully charge

---

[1] Notably including the growing tide of foreign bribery cases, as well as the high-profile Ponzi schemes of Bernard Madoff and others.

[2] See Ethics Resource Center 2007 press release announcing the results of the 2007 National Business Ethics Survey, available at http://eon.businesswire.com/portal/site/eon/permalink/ ?ndmViewId=news_view&newsId=20071128105353&newsLang=en.

the power of these programs. This paper offers a series of ideas and suggestions for further steps that government could take along these lines.

What Policy Options Might Government Consider?

1.   Issue enforcement policy statements that recognize the importance of empowered CECOs in corporate compliance efforts. Enforcement policies could take into account company compliance programs with empowered CECOs in any decision to prosecute. The Holder, Thompson and McNulty memos and ultimately the U.S. Attorneys' Manual are examples of relevant policy statements that could be revised to flesh out the need for empowered CECOs. This enforcement policy could be visibly implemented by criminal enforcement authorities and regulatory agencies. Public pronouncements by government officials promoting these sorts of empowerment steps could also be a positive influence.

The more specific the government is in its commitment to CECOs as an element of effective corporate compliance, the more impact the government is likely to have on this point. For example, in Canada the Canadian Competition Bureau (CCB) has offered an example of how the need for CECO empowerment can be articulated.[3]

2.   Publicize the benefits of strong leadership in compliance and ethics programs. Government could seek to publicize specific instances in which a compliance program with an empowered CECO results in a benefit to a company. Providing examples of the benefits, and of what the government expects to see in strong ethics and compliance programs, has the potential to magnify the impact of the government's policy in this area. In particular, this is one way that government might offer the private sector a "carrot," to complement the "stick" of criminal enforcement activity.

3.   Establish practical, flexible standards for the CECO role. Government could write more detailed, practical but flexible standards for CECO empowerment in companies. By giving guidance for what is expected, but leaving room for companies to customize the CECO role for their own circumstances, companies would then have the incentive to undertake realistic assessment of what they need to do to improve. Again, the FSGO set an example for the kind of guidance that can be offered here. The best standards

---

[3] The Canadian Competition Bureau (CCB) offered a strongly articulated guidance on the importance of CECOs to criminal enforcement efforts: "Irrespective of the size and the resources of a particular business, the person or group responsible for compliance must act effectively in that there is a need for independence, professionalism, empowerment, financial support and a solid understanding of what is taking place within the business." See http://www.competitionbureau.gc.ca/eic/site/cb-bc.nsf/vwapj/Compliance-Bulletin-090808-Final-e.pdf/$FILE/Compliance-Bulletin-090808-Final-e.pdf.

provide enough specificity to be predictable, but enough flexibility to allow innovation and constant improvement.

4.   Incorporate reference to CECOs into requirements for government procurement. The federal government has recently imposed a compliance program requirement on most government contractors.   That requirement could easily be modified to emphasize the importance of an empowered CECO as an element of a satisfactory compliance program.

5.   Incorporate reference to CECOs in deferred prosecution agreements, corporate integrity agreements, and other settlements.   The government could include CECO empowerment in all settlement arrangements with companies.[4]

6.   Revise the Federal Sentencing Guidelines.   Reference to the role of CECOs, and standards for what the CECO role in ethics and compliance programs should involve, could be incorporated into an amended version of the FSGO.

7.   Other regulatory agencies could address the potential role of CECOs in addressing specific areas of risk and compliance.   CECO empowerment potentially could be encouraged in programs in a number of regulatory areas beyond criminal prosecution, e.g., in the context of environmental regulation, financial services regulation, healthcare regulation, etc.   Each regulatory or enforcement agency can consider the best ways to address CECO empowerment in their own guidance documents.

8.   Encourage stock exchanges to consider the role of the CECO.   Government could encourage stock exchanges to include as a company listing requirement the designation of a CECO, with well-defined powers and adequate resources attached to the role.   Such a requirement would complement the existing exchange requirements for company codes of conduct — and would likely be more effective in helping to drive improved ethics and compliance programs within companies.

9.   Factor the role of CECOs in administering voluntary disclosure programs. Regulators could include effective programs with empowered CECOs as a factor for lenient treatment in voluntary disclosure programs.   Typically, voluntary disclosure programs set certain conditions for inclusion in agency leniency policies.   Having an effective compliance program, or agreeing to undertake one, could be added to this list.   The existence of such a

---

[4] For model DPA language referring to CECOs, see Murphy, "How DPAs, CIAs and Other Settlements Can Have a Lasting Effect," *ethikos*, Vol. 21, No. 9 (May/June 2008).

program could also be used in assessing any other required elements in the disclosure requirements for lenient treatment.

10. <u>Consider reducing regulatory requirements for companies with strong compliance programs and empowered CECOs</u>. Reducing the regulatory burden offers another potential type of "carrot" for companies that empower their CECOs and enact strong ethics and compliance programs. One analogy might be OSHA's Voluntary Protection Program model, in which participating companies are subject to reduced frequency of OSHA inspections. In the compliance and ethics context, participating companies might be offered expedited treatment from the government (e.g., licenses, applications, etc.), reduced regulatory fees, or some other set of regulatory benefits.

11. <u>Consider establishing the relevance of CECOs in compliance programs as a defense to civil liability</u>. In principle, legislative reform could help establish empowered CECOs and strong compliance programs as a partial defense to civil liability, e.g., the model in the Ellerth case[5] for harassment claims. For example, in any civil claim where organizational intent is at issue, the existence of an ethics and compliance program with an empowered CECO could be offered as evidence of the company's intent to do the right thing.

12. <u>Consider the CECO role as a defense for directors' liability</u>. Policymakers might consider legislation to establish a due diligence defense for corporate directors who institute effective programs. In jurisdictions where board members could otherwise face civil or criminal liability for organizational misconduct, the existence of an effective compliance program and the board's empowerment and oversight of the CECO could be made determinative of such individual liability, following the Caremark case[6] model.

13. <u>Encourage extension of the CECO role through the supply chain</u>. Regulators could include in their standards for CECOs and compliance programs the requirement that companies in turn encourage or require their suppliers to institute programs with empowered CECOs. This is a step that could help extend the trend toward better ethics and compliance efforts to smaller companies.

14. <u>Offer tax credits</u>. The government could consider offering tax credits for companies that implement effective compliance programs, and particularly for meeting the criterion of empowered CECOs. A tax credit would provide a very specific, measurable incentive to

---

[5] Burlington Industries, Inc. v. Ellerth, 524 U.S. 742 (1998)

[6] In re Caremark International Inc. Derivative Litigation, 698 A.2d 959 (Del. Ch. 1996)

companies in all fields to adopt related programs, and even a one-time credit for companies to initiate such programs could have an effect.

15. <u>Establish conditions for access to government bailout money</u>. When the government provides taxpayer money to private businesses in distress, it should take reasonable steps to ensure the money is handled appropriately. Government could readily require any recipient of bailout funds to agree to implement a state-of-the-art compliance and ethics program, with a powerful CECO charged with protecting the taxpayers' money.

16. <u>Participate actively in compliance and ethics conferences</u>.
Government representatives could take on a more active role in participating in compliance organization conferences and seminars. Too often, government officials are absent from these settings, or appear only to speak and then rush away. Active engagement by government officials in these sorts of meetings could provide further support for empowering CECOs and compliance programs, while also promoting useful exchange of information between government and private-sector actors.

17. <u>Provide training for government officials</u>. Enforcement and regulatory officials could be offered training in the compliance field, to learn better how to assess program effectiveness and why the CECO is such a key player. While government personnel have training and background in enforcement activities, they often lack expertise in the compliance area. Greater familiarity and sophistication could be useful in myriad ways both to ongoing government enforcement efforts and to any future efforts to identify and reward superior performers in compliance and ethics.

18. <u>Promote corporate compliance initiatives as a measure by which government oversight efforts are assessed</u>. In particular, agencies' activities in promoting corporate compliance programs could be assessed as an indicator of regulatory performance, in favor of simple accumulation of enforcement or prosecution numbers. For example, successes might be measured in such figures as the number of voluntary disclosures by companies, number of regulated companies with strong compliance programs and empowered CECOs, etc.

19. <u>Work against anti-compliance actions and rulings</u>. Certain government actions and court decisions actually discourage or undermine compliance programs and CECO empowerment. Enforcement authorities and regulators should be vigilant against efforts to undercut compliance programs, including litigants' schemes to exploit company compliance efforts through the legal system. Government should also promote protections for bona fide compliance activities (e.g., statutory defenses to defamation claims from company compliance disciplinary cases).

20. <u>Establish legal protection for corporate compliance efforts</u>. The risk of having compliance efforts used against a company in discovery and litigation can be a substantial deterrent for companies.[7] Agencies might ameliorate the risk by adopting policies against seeking or using such materials against companies with empowered CECOs. Alternately, legislation could establish a strong privilege and immunity for such materials.

21. <u>Provide a role model of a robust compliance and ethics approach: government agency compliance programs</u>. Ideally, the various federal agencies could institute their own compliance programs as a model for what such programs should look like in the private sector. The current model in some governmental units — comprised of an OIG "police officer" and an ethics officer focused on technical conflicts of interest rules — does not approach the level of a fully empowered ethics and compliance program per the Federal Sentencing Guidelines standard.

22. <u>Collaborate with international organizations</u>. Government could work with international organizations (e.g., the EU, OECD) to try to extend regulatory approaches to corporate ethics and compliance internationally. For example, the OECD anti-corruption treaty and follow-up OECD initiatives might be amended to incorporate specific incentives for compliance programs with empowered CECOs.

23. <u>Evaluate the drawbacks, as well as the advantages, of mandatory compliance programs</u>. Arguably, the trend to mandate compliance programs or program elements has sometimes had unintended and undesirable consequences. For example, Sarbanes-Oxley and the stock exchange listing requirements have elevated company codes of conduct to an artificial status that may be well beyond what they deserve, while the same requirements have neglected to address the need for empowered compliance and ethics leadership. Mandating programs and specific features may also have the unintended effect of promoting legalistic responses and counterproductive resistance to what is perceived as government intrusion.[8] Ideally, government should consult with compliance and ethics experts as a precursor to such efforts, in order to avoid or minimize the likelihood of perverse results. The value of using incentives, rather than compulsion, should be considered before resort to compulsion.

24. <u>Designate an official in charge</u>. Government agencies could act to designate an official as their formal compliance and ethics liaison, with primary responsibility for promoting effective compliance and ethics programs, including empowered CECOs.

---

[7] See Murphy, "Compliance on Ice: How Litigation Chills Compliance Programs," *Corporate Conduct Quarterly*, Vol. 2, No. 36 (Winter 1992) (now *ethikos*).

[8] See Murphy, "Mandavolent Compliance," *ethikos*, Vol. 19, No. 8 (Sept/Oct 2005).

25. <u>Establish credible program assessment</u>. Government could play an important role in establishing a credible, consistent framework for assessing corporate compliance programs. We have offered a number of suggestions for governmental incentives, tied to the existence of an effective compliance program with an empowered CECO. Reasonable, explicit assessment criteria are a prerequisite for the government to administer any of these kinds of incentives.

<u>Conclusion</u>

As the foregoing list makes clear, there is a great deal the government potentially could do to promote more effective corporate ethics and compliance programs, and in particular to empower the CECO as an agent of change. We respectfully suggest that the empowerment of CECOs might be a particularly cost-effective method for government to use in this area, because it leverages off of the ability of companies to self-police. The compliance and ethics profession stands ready to assist in this mission.

REFERENCES

Association of Certified Fraud Examiners (2008), *2008 Report to the Nation on Occupational Fraud and Abuse*. As of April 1, 2009:
http://www.whistleblowers.nonprofitsoapbox.com/storage/whistleblowers/ documents/acfefraudreport.pdf

Ethics Resource Center (2003), "Focus on the National Business Ethics Survey 2003." *Ethics Today On-Line*, Vol. 1, June 2003. As of April 1, 2009:
http://www.ethics.org/erc-publications/ethics-today.asp?aid=733

Ethics Resource Center (2007), *National Business Ethics Survey 2007*. Arlington, VA: Ethics Resource Center.

PricewaterhouseCoopers (2007), *Economic Crime, People and Controls: The 4th Biennial Global Economic Crime Survey*. As of April 1, 2009:
http://www.whistleblowers.org/storage/whistleblowers/documents/ pwc_survey.pdf

Thompson, Larry D. (2003). "Principles of Federal Prosecution of Business Organizations." January 20th Memorandum to Heads of Department Components, United States Attorneys. Washington, D.C.: Office of the Deputy Attorney General, United States Department of Justice. As of April 1, 2009:
www.usdoj.gov/dag/cftf/corporate_guidelines.htm

U.S. Sentencing Commission (undated). "Organizational Guidelines." As of March 2009:
http://www.ussc.gov/orgguide.htm